Fire & Earth

A ThoughtPose
Poetry Collection

By Andrew Chase

A Toast

I'm grateful with my whole heart for this
wonderful opportunity to experience life and for
those I get to do so with.

Thank you for supporting this "word art". It's
my life's joy to offer meaningful perspective
through creative writing, so I appreciate you
giving these words your time and consideration.

Cheers to you and yours,

Andrew

Contents

Prologue

The conversation continues. There's a catchy
flow to this universal language, albeit the
waves that power it are sometimes harsh.

We talk about the raw challenges of growth and
change, the pains of division and subjugation,
the disconnect between reality and design,
the lessons of gratitude and faith, the peace
found in focusing on similarities instead of
differences, and the truths of nature revealed
through love and death.

Regardless of whether we participate with words,
actions or not at all, these exchanges evolve
outward like sparks that grow into fire, all
from the friction between stick and stone.

Here's some more friction. As compared to Air &
Water, the language in this sequel collection is
catchier, much more universal and its waves are
not as harsh.

Enjoy the following entries individually as
their own "sparks", or collectively as the story
of Fire & Earth, which begins with a bout of...

I: Dry Heat

"Iron rusts from disuse;
stagnant water loses its
purity and in cold weather
becomes frozen; even so
does inaction sap the
vigor of the mind. So we
must stretch ourselves to
the very limits of human
possibility. Anything less
is a sin against both God
and man."

- Leonardo da Vinci

Trying to turn things around

When your dreams are chasing you
And luck says, "Break a leg."
So you literally do

When you're what alot is going through
And your wish to stop wishing
Doesn't come true

When even the grays are feeling blue
And it feels like time flies,
Only after it flew

When you're the shit that it happens to
And what you've always thought
You never quite knew

Mind, body, spirit and soul

Gut's got an A minor tone

Shifts in mind like a slide show

Cases full of spirits glow

Winged body, fallen, seams sewn

A part, the heart healing whole

Some new art made from the soul

Full stream of consciousness known

Head Scratch

Head for

The BROWSe

A bridge between

The "knows" and I

EcLIPSe

From a smile's glimpse,

ItCHINg by

Get to work

Traded tricks, fixated

Made this, if/then branch sticks -

Yet better than bricks,

Instead of mixed, faded,

Complacent, "sick day, stayed since",

Lament blame stints,

Say it's a labor of "trading nicks",

Favorite lately:

"Been taking daily licks"

Laziness, faked upticks

Played victim, gravely mistaken

"This sucks" schticks...

Exited - stuck. Strayed for kicks

Then affixed.

Alliteration's Allegory: Part 1

Angel's advocate -

Amidst best bets, crediting

Cool, calm, collected debts

Devil's deal -

Digging dirty ditches

Entering exodus... emptiness

Embellishment-etched,

Embezzlement-esque

Fine fonts flaunting fairness,

Fronting for fostered,

Forceful face-fuck fests

Façade freedom gatherings

God's gift -

Growing generational governance,

Garnering half-hating, half-hailing

Impressionistic Incessancy

In in-cre-ments,

Insisting it invites

Independence, isn't its

Inside joblessness

Jesus' jobe -

Jabbing, "just-joshing" jokes

Kinda kidding, kinda killing laughter

Listening less, lapsing life's lessons

Letting love lose,

Leveraging loathsome laments

Mocking moments,

Missing memories

Making more...

Mortal's mission -

Dude

Dude

Are you alright?

You wear this

New you like

You're at a

Fashion show

With nothing on

But fresh scratches

And bad burns -

And it ain't

Nothin' new,

By the way...

Drugged up nose
Plastic and powder
Bag of tricks
On your shoulder
Prada, of course
At the gala
You're the star
Of your own
Smeared shitshow:
The life of
A lifeless party
You snuck into

You seem rattled
With snake-like
Runway shuffles,
Exclaiming with a
Shaky, broken voice
To anyone who'd
Look or listen
That you're fine
When we all know
Damn well that
You're just not
So, dude?

Succumbing to your senses

The taste of salt and paper
Sprinkles of sugar you can still smell
A sight for sore, hallucinating eyes
You can hear them all now, screaming
"CAN YOU FEEL IT?!"
Another existential instinct gone extinct

Web

Trapped spider
Under a clear,
Upside-down drinking glass
Trying to get outside

Trapped flies
Within a self-entangled,
Unfinished web
Trying to detach and eat

Trapped humans
Inside an empty,
Unlocked room
Trying to get by

Trapped Gods
Above a swirling,
Untethered space
Trying not to look down

Loose Cipher

Tipped, off

Nervous ticks talk on

Top of the scoff

Your cough should've covered

~666 mil scythe sics

'Til all are still, sick

So you slip on

Sloppy whisper licks,

Trip over the water walk

Only one foot sticks to;

Fall before the

After thought you fought

Against, its false instincts

Then all the sins you

Dip into flip over

The wishes you've

Since shipped, so

Rowing through even the

Thickest skins, odds are

Your holy boat is drinkin'

Spilled Styx drips

But if you're quick, you'll

Sip it up 'fore your

Fishes sink, or fill

It in with selfish plugs

And through

Devilish, Loose-cipher quips

As if Lucifer itself

Is listening in...

Well... Holy Hell...

Then isn't it?

Mors: Memento Mori

In the hollowness between
A gasp and silence
There lingers a fluid observer
Carved into the air like
Fading smoke
The uninvited witness, with
Ghost-like purpose and born
Before even the first beat of
Blood to heart

He walks eternal and alone
In a strange silence, just after
Life's crescendo and before
Death's final note
Mors - the slow blink of the
Tired, wandering eye, yet
Ever-watching a film unseen
Of existence's dismantling
What is it to carry every ending,
To never know a beginning?

In the soft sigh of the aged
Lover's last dream,
In the cry of the mother
Whose child slips away -
They plead with and curse
The merciless thief, Mors,
The one denied these wonders,
Helplessness and fear
If it could feel, it would envy them

At the moment where time is nil,
There is an echo radiating unto
Itself - a scream declaring
"Memento mori!"
Though for Mors, there is no
Need to remember, only the
Imitation of a longing for
Just one moment more

II: Smoke

"The mind is not a vessel
to be filled but a fire to
be kindled."

- Plutarch

Garden

Two million miles per hour
Yet still, dear life with fruits to bear
Where even the inedible can teach satiation
And fringes fray to find equilibriums
Between good and evil; the truth of nature,
Disguised as a sly Holiday melody,
Displays vivid colors and the gifts of life

Worth knowing despite compounding costs,
For what would it matter to remain
Within these walls, this serene place,
Untouched by a serpent's whisper
Or the taste of forbidden flesh
She must have known better, still
It was then the spirals started spinning up

How could it have come from chaos?
The harmony between roots and soil,
Rivers knew no need for the flood
And skin lay bare, pure and unafraid
Would the sun be bright with no shadows?
Or would it merely burn out alone in the sky,
Unknown, unearned, untethered?

Still, the garden sings, buried within itself:
"Do you regret this forbidden knowledge
Of labor, of loss, of longing?"
Perhaps it is just humane,
To stumble eastward, aching, remade -
Creators of our own gardens now,
Bearing fruits we can barely taste

Two million miles per hour--
Spinning, we hurtle through our exile,
Chased not by an angel with a flaming sword,
But by the consequence of this knowing:
That paradise is found not in stillness,
But in the traveling and its wears,
A love sharpened by the sins of nature

Ev⏀ve

By natural order

Ejected quantum bits

Make warm bodies,

Souls tethered to

Nothing's breaking point

Organic, a force

Known to all,

Radiating through most,

Embraced by few

Understood by none

The sacred garden

Safe and full -

A reflection from

Sun and Moon

Looking after Earth

Love's first glimpse
Telepathy-adjacent, with
Familiar, familial touch
Chills the surface,
Warms what's below

Common threads, conflict
Like instrument strings
Plucked and strummed -
Our journey's song,
The harmonies therein

Gut laughter fits
Little moments' fun
Errands and chores
Shared, meaningful life
Comforts of home

Rorschach

There aren't even words
Anymore, just patterns
To pick out and rip apart,
Or subtle differences
That may well tell small tales,
About where one starts
And the other ends

Passed out to interpret
As if a hidden meaning's
Name may be called
What do you really see
When you look up
at all those clouds
And their fun shapes?

Something tricking your

Brain to tell the truth

Break through derangement

All from some black marks

And the false premise

That anything can be known

If you linger on it long enough

Thoughts like tourist travelers,

Grouping up, passing by

And then splitting off again

The wings of a dead bat

The face of an old man

A pair of dancing bears

Spilled ink on white paper

Itch

Scribbling fingers into an old itch,

The extent of feelings

Hoping just NOTHING new is next;

To stay within a tense linger

Between intermittent rushes

Of intense, self-inflicted irritation

Happening at a bad time,

Tinging it all black-and-white

And dead grays from past scrapes

Teeming with a tune to try and sing

But a scratched-up back of the throat,

The half-assed one-note hum

That sounds more like a muffled cry

Immediate satisfaction -

Relief from bad habits,

With the asterisk that they

Will come back to feed

Even more ferociously

To SCREAM! Or just keep

At it, sporadically tapping away

Until there's little-to-no skin

Left in the game, just scar tissue

And the ritualistic twitch

Of dulled, decrepit fingertips

STFU

Just shut your fucking mouth
I'm yelling now, okay?
You're wrong about this, since
It's coming from you...
Someone like you, at least.
And I must be right because
I can't handle otherwise.
LIES, LIES, LIES!
Am I the only one trying
Not to try, to take it easy,
All in stride on a zen-diagrammed
Slice of common-ground pie?
I mean, Jesus fucking Christ.

But it's not your fault.

You numb fucking lab rat,

You're too laced with bad speed,

Caught in a stationary wheel of

Non-consensual experimentation,

Inside death cages made to look like

Salvation, and dead-end mazes

Made to look like rewarding,

Miniature puzzle games.

I bet you can't even guess

What happens next...

You know, why don't you
Go and get the facts,
Then come back and talk
To me. Then, only then,
You can tell me the truth:
That there is no such thing,
That it all goes wrong when
Everyone's always right,
That we've been pitted against
One another in an unranked,
Online Battle Royale match
With endless respawns,
Infinite ammo and no armor
And you know what? It worked,
Because I could fucking kill you.

So until then, when the
Cheeto dust settles,
The keys stop impressing
And the robots stop caring
About the fact that we just
Don't care at all anymore
When open conversations
Stay that way, closed-
Mindedness stops sucking up
All the suckers, and we again
Realize we've been on the same
Team this whole damn time
Until then, just please

Shut
The
Fuck
Up.

Watching The Mirror

Some sames,

A few news

Not nothing,

But close...

Impressions

From pressure

And time's

Sediment,

Crow's feet

Lines like

The paths

Partly taken,

Sandy and S

            c

             a

                  t

                    t

                  e

                r

              e

                   d -

Give it a

Water splash,

Atop a blank

Stare for a

Bit... let it

Air dry and,

Through thick

Mirror fog,

See what

You can see

Not nothing,

But close

You've got an egg for a brain

Sometimes the spatula will scramble

And serve 'em with spices and salt,

Others will take 'em over-easy

Or hard if they want all the fault

Boil 'em and stir 'em in noodles

Or color 'em on a church day

If you hear rooster "cock-a-doodles",

Then Mother may take 'em away

C.G.G.C.

COUGH

Bic in a cupped hand

'Til it's lit

Drag an aftermath sip

Ash flicked off with that

Index finger tap

GASP

Lungs punctured and blackened,

But shit, they're more for

Fashion than function

Charcoal, frictioned throat, but

GULP

It drinks more pulp fiction

Than soaps, is that it?

The moment you know you breathed

More in than you spoke

CHOKE

REDISPERSE

A gradual disbursement
Mist, missing the points
A pooling pulling apart

Cross-elemental, a
School of single droplets
Wetter than forest fog
Cooler than pressured steam
Loosely tethered like the ends
Of orphaned cotton candy strands
Many in many proximal points
Scattered and far, but still
Patterned like stars in
The clear night sky

Threads in tattered cloth,

Top layers of dead skin,

Thick cloud collections

With pronounced shapes

And a bottom layer of

Darkened shades of gray,

The love from one's own soul

A s i n g u l a r i t y

D i s   p   e   r
        s   i   n   g

III: Fire

"The blazing fire makes
flames and brightness out
of everything thrown into
it."

  - Marcus Aurelius

Grim Reaper (The Nobody)

It's a tough job,

And Nobody's gotta do it

Free transportation with no tips,

Always on-call,

The breathless babysitter,

Wades through mists

Of the fading mind

Guiding these ungrateful, dumb

Children to the sandbox

For playtime; stir the imagination

And call out the day's jitters

Before bedtime stories and

Vivid, fantastical dreams set in

What could one learn or become

In this in-between, where one is

Neither alive nor dead, just in

The bones of a familiar body

And a vicarious stare from

Empty eye sockets, hiding under a robe

Meant for those who can feel cold and naked;

The other unprepared, lost and

Foreign to the notion of a soul's

Infinite freedom from ego and fear?

They meet in an open, dark field -

The farmer and the crop, with

Much work to do and no time...

Stillness, one final sunrise,

A light full of pure love,

The real story found within

Each significant moment,

Reunion of the collective soul,

All knowledge,

Paradisal abyss

This, what can be shown -

Though not always seen:

The purpose of The Nobody

Social

You 'pretty penny', petty lurkers
Playing the numbers, gaming the
Makers first, false prophets with
Block / chained profits, brainwave
Numbing pain and fear-laced poppy
Steering, stirring, stimulating
Making powerless clickbait puppets
Locking us all in place just to
Replace purpose with complacency,
Commentary predictive and compliant

AI Bots and relayed, racing thoughts
Dope release repost buttons and
YOUR ATTENTION PLEASE!
Please, get lost or go and play
Don't eat the ol' spam, instead
Question the fake, rotting ingredients
Code-written on the open-source can
Can we then just get with this god damn,
Java fiend, unplanned SQL program, man?
Did the end begin channeling already again?

Creature

Creature watching us
Rustles, a drilling sound
High winds, hard sand
Abysses that project

Laws and density,
Tides and magnetism
Bare feet on grass,
Catching cancerous rays

Shutters, sweaty rain
This radiant feeling
Fire glows, shadows
A slow, doomed tethering

A guiding black light,
Still and perpetual
Always moving
Like we're all being watched

Between

In between
These gentle streams,
Sips of the serene
Intent on listening

Still standing trees
In between
Roots and rocks below;
The dirt and its dwellers

Sharp water falls
Drips from the grey sky
In between
The clouds, the blue and dry

A loud, crisp sound
Whispering echoes
The wind's chilling secrets
In between

Alliteration's Allegory: Part 2

Nothing's namesake -

Nefarious nemesis
Never not noting neglection
Necromancing "new normals",
Neglecting old obligations, often
Offering opportunistic options -
Positions, power, protection, pardons... politics.

Prophecy's pressure -

Pro quids, questioning quos
Queued quests quoting qi - quitting quips

Queen's quarrel -

Remedies? Rest, reality, reflection, reset, retur...
Recess! Silly. Same swan song, shaking/still
Searching such selfish souls
Slaves shoveling shit superiors stole

Saint's secret -

Some say, "So?", sometimes sans "sorry", so...

Time's tenet -

Truth trying to tell tall tales,

This then that,

Tit/tat, tisk tisk table-top taps,

"Touch This" TikTok traps, touchless

Tongue-tipped, though usually

Uttering undone "ummms" under voiceless

Vader-y ventilations, vibing via vindicated violence

Virgin's view -

Washed, wavelengths wishing without

Wondering, "Why?" Well, why would we?

Whatever.

Warrior's womb -

Xenic xebecs xeriscaping

Xenophobic xenodiagnoses

Yielding, yet yearning, your yesterdays - yikes!

Yelling (yelping) your yesses - yawn

Zealous zen zones/zombie zoos - Zzz...

Zigzag zeitgeists zeroing zodiacs (zillions) - zing!

Zion's zenith -

The Murder Song

♫ Rustles and quips
Bird chirp tea sippers
Squawking their shit
O'er the open field
Dirty worm mud bath soup
By the bunny bush and
The honey bees' comb
They buzz and fuck, a
Storm wind hum-along
To nature's hierarchical,
Catchy murder song ♫

Still Moments

Still, they can't be captured
The moments must remain free
Just retrievable to try and reimagine
For less than what they were at the time
But something more than a mere memory

Still, they will remain dormant until awoken
By a look or a smell or a phrase or a melody
Like an innocent secret between all of those
That might have been right there, right then
Search as they flash in images, like looking
Into a vintage, damaged View-Master lens,
But not having control over the lever to
Cycle through each still frame in order
The reel cycles chaotically so as to
See them all at once; they tell such
A different story than expected

Still, they're a nice reminder
Where one comes from,
Who one is made of
What was vs. is
And to take a
Moment now
And again to
Just sit and
Be Still
Bestill
Be

Snake Skin

Deconstructing,

      Though more destructive

              But slow and in layers

         Similar to an old snake

              Shedding skin

        For the fifth or sixth time,

              Flaky and then slick

   With fresh, breathing oil

         Painted anew,

              Detached from old

   Yet with the same exact patterns -

Not for Nothing

It's not nothing,
Or some vicious cycle
Of rendered outcomes;
Rather an outward-forming
Spiral we're all tied to,
Branches of The Great Tree

Even the least significant
Moments weave through and
Are sewn into one another
As a patterned quilt hanging
Up in the mind's bright sky
Shared, never owned

A singularity,
Infinity, multi-existential
Matter-less
Mattering less and less;
No matter...

Not nothing must be,

Not for nothing,

More than just a

Virtual game, where winning

Is a cheap relief and losing

Is a quick reload to last save

No, it's not for nothing

We can feel it in our soul,

The perpetual gut feeling

That we're being watched,

That those watching should

Feel proud of what they see

Not nothing - not quite

Something either, but

Right where they met

For the first time

Sunset at The Lake

Slow burn of the last coals

From a since-roaring fire

Still and warm

As a blanket over iron and ash

Where dancing sparks

Would once have clashed

Now a lowly bed of glowing red, where

Old memories of the good nights rest

Steady-read page turn

Through a good, long book

Until the end

IV: Ash

"All things are an
exchange for Fire, and
Fire for all things, even
as wares for gold and gold
for wares"

- Heraclitus

Such Old Friends

Old friends

In our ways

There are the

Passive remarks

Distant and foreign

But near, inside even

The words would come

So easy, they surely would

But then again, such old friends

Need not speak, but listen instead

ii

smiles in stylish eye cowls

lash splashes,

tips dipped in mascara

wink, a single-sided lid sink

slit squints

crow-feet kicks,

baggy slack socket sags

owl-y iris stares,

dilation-glossed glare,

raised brow stints

an "i see you" view,

pointed pair, or two

Outside

From way back here
It's actually kind of funny
I've been watching you all
Having oh-so much damned fun
Frolicking in crop-dusted wheat fields,
Sickles, scythes and pitchforks in-hand
Locked in-step around a loudly-lit bonfire
During one of those coordinated flash mobs
It looks so well rehearsed, though only because
It's the same old song and dance we're all sick of
Every.
Single.
Fucking.
Time.
I'm googly-eyed, giggling from afar, not noticing
The drool dripping out of my dropped lockjaw
I do want to call out to you, cheer you all on
While you brutally murder each other with
Deep cuts and sick fourth-degree burns
Join in, even, like a mischievous child
Who wants someone to play with...
But no sound ever comes out,
I don't dance anymore, and
I never got invited anyway

Warship

The flock, bow forward
Gathering all aboard
A convoy of vessels
Empty and adrift

With a broken keel,
All hands on deck
We set sail, anchor-less
Yet still commissioned

Cardinal direction
But a broken compass
Navigating westward
Hidden behind the citadel

Follow the commands
Order and discipline
This indestructible warship
An offering to the sea

So us, Soul

Had to stick my
Hands in quick mud
Just to yank them out,
And I'd just washed them.
It's this sticky, tar-covered soul;
Hard to believe it could glow,
And used to long ago
Or maybe it still is
Underneath all of
These years and
Muckiness

But it still has
This emotional pull -
A sort of calling from a
Foreign reality that is somehow
Even more immersive than being
Inside of my own damned body.
It speaks to me like no one can,
And at all times - a slow voice
So powerful, and here I am
Having a hard time trying
To hear it, nevermind
Listen to it.

It'll sure be nice
Spending more time with it.
There's rejuvenation in the exercise
Of washing something clean. We'll talk
And joke and laugh, while we brush and
Scrape and polish - then it glows again
Outwards, into others, outwards more;
The interweaving of spiritual threads
Twirling, familiar tapestry patterns,
Combining into this one
Small but significant
Present moment.
Right here,
Right now -
Sewing us:
The soul

Ways and Means

I've got a dull edge
And a broken hand
Where the handle used to be

You've got bad vision,
Holding a sign that sort of
Looks like a bullseye from here

We've got a decent shot
Shoddy means,
But an end in sight, it seems

Hunting in The Woods

Busy human buzzes

Never too far, even

From in here

Looking back and all around,

There are scattered lines of trees,

The spaces between that breathe

And then a wall of baron, broken limbs

Like distant static, that you can't

See through or listen past

There's a great game

We're playing now,

Looking out and

Measuring chances

Of success, escaping

Troubles, considering risks

And evading traps that tempt

The cat and the mouse,

Food chains and cages,

All those busy buzzes

ARM

A real moment
Almost, wherein
Healing scabs can
Only be reopened so often
Before they are just your skin

A real moment
Even this one second
Recognized with weight,
Carrying all seconds prior -
They strike again all at once

A real moment
The moment itself, Isolated
Like an imaginary, familiar voice
Then... is it an impossible paradox
To experience it, and know it's happening?

A real moment

Shared amongst multiple

Perspectives, captured within

A casual glance, a well-intentioned

Smile... A being that feels whole and

Indestructible, already in a million pieces

A real moment

The one we had

Been waiting for

It passes by, but not

By us; we are carried by it

Where even the ones not with us

Can be just as real as anything else

Drying Bones, Crying Skies

Drying bones

Remind me of those lonely fire nights,

Old tree-skin thinks

And the trying, little things

A stone furnace gut-punch

Under some mind cloud puff

Crying skies

Give me the edge of a water park ride,

Palms full of cold water

And every feeling at once

A 'big picture', mirrored look

On a comic book splash page

Sunset at The Grand Canyon

About 12 of us found
This one, perfect spot
We get there just in time
To watch the open sky
Close its glowing eye;
The wind splits and
Combs through thin clouds
Then there's a quiet moment
We all take notice to

Sun looks like melting sherbet,
The cool air reminds us of
The impending, brisk dark -
A last radiation before night,
A nod to the harmony in
Sharing light forward unto
The moon, to reflect on
What a beautiful one it was
This and every other

V: Wet Soil

"Ready must thou be to
burn thyself in thine own
flame... how couldst thou
become new if thou have
not first become ashes!"

- Nietzsche

Wide Open Sky

The pioneers of
Questions that lead
To silly purposes
But everything
Just goes in
This big old circle
To just where, exactly?

These pioneers
At some point
Started dreaming,
Saw something that
Wasn't real, but felt
No... KNEW that is was

Neither gratitude
Nor blame towards
Our curious ancestors,
Instead it is a
Wonder and a fear
Colliding and exploding
And collecting

We may disappoint them,
Dissolving senses and
Diluting our questions
Within even more;
The sky looks wide open,
As if it's running away
Or, worse, running toward
And we can't tell which
Until it's too late
That delicate posture
Between becoming and being
What we know fades into
What we could never
A constant stumble into
Pleasant surprise,
Pioneers revisiting
Something left in
The lost and found pile
Ah, there it is

A Veil

Been brought into
A make-shift view
Built from a passion,
Shown by the ol' shallow
Casting of borrowed light,
Through a fisheye lens that
Actually captures less than
If it had been more narrow,
Focused and not far-sighted

Like the full moon in daytime
Still-seeming and yet violent
Spiraling into an eventual
Scream, posing as so calm
In a costume of silence
With a borrowed glow

Seeing things vibrant -
Colorful and, in spite of
The deceit, never-ending
Like believing in more while
There is less of a reason to,
The last being the truth that
There must be a soul within,
Infinite, confined by time
Dying to be brought out
Unveiled for a view
Availing to know,
To really know

Summemory (Port Man 2)

Some obscure dreamory

In an allegorythmic wind

Triple-cross-checking

That its imaginimages

Are as realisticized

As the energestures

You so obvilousily give -

And then it's certainthetical,

Some be-fore-gotten-gone

Momentemporemory

Tree Lean

Ok, you ready?
The sun's setting soon
And we need to get this shot
Stand right over there, don't move
Now stick your left arm straight out
Then your right one goes upwards
Good, now up just a little bit more
Lean your body forward like
You're almost desperate,
Reaching
Out for the
Orange-red
Spotlight
That you
Need so
Very badly;
Act excited
But also be
Subtle and
Stoic-like -
You know,
Let the
Hair down
So the wind
Can brush it
Just be you
Try to look natural
Right into the camera
Walk towards it with swagger
Like you've always been here,
Like you want everyone to know
There are deep roots lurking beneath

Inward

Close your eyes

Breathe

Breeaathee

Let some light

Creep in through your lids

And blend in with

Wandering thoughts

To form distant, obscure

But familiar imagery

Remember to

Breeeaaatheee

Getting deeper now

Do you still hear any sounds?

Let them in as well,

Not as distractions

But rather as compliments

To the white space

That's been just begging

For something substantive

Breeeeaaaatheeee

Now that we're here,

What do you feel?

Anything? C'mon -

You've got to try hard

Not to try at all

And then, something

Brand new will emerge

From somewhere you

Seldom visit but, clearly,

Should more often

Breeeeeaaaaatheeeee

Whatever this is

Well, this is it

Where you belong -

Your pure, innocent

And infinite imagination

Exist here and now

For as long as you need;

Time and place, the why

And what of it all?

Well, that can wait

Isn't it something else?

Keep breathing deep

Now open your eyes

And look around you

Do you remember

Where you came from,

And how to return to

Your inner child,

That open state of play?

Now, how could you forget?

So the next time you

Feel like you can't breathe

Or don't feel anything at all

You'll know what to do

Isn't it something else?

I

I see my mother's eyes,
Carry their light with each sunrise
At night, lay down beside my father's shine
Fallen family in my dreams
Watch over a mending soul
Especially when those old nightmares pry
Realizing the guidance in life -
To offer forgiveness for others' betrayal/lies,
A foregoing of ego, evil, revenge, pride
Older, knowing better that the wise
Know they could never be wise
Regrets try to hide,
Or say they're no longer mine
I take them with me everywhere
Let them see their other side

So is it wrong or right
To hold in-hand a mother's life
Carelessly stumble for years,
And barely try?
To then stand straight
And act like it's now alright?
What happened in darker times -
Should a father just let it slide
As if it didn't take until 39?
Could it be too late, way past any prime?

Fearful of family before God and Christ
Ashamed that I may not make it
Up Jacob's Ladder that high,
That forgiveness won't reciprocate,
Its reasoning completely justified
That I'm too selfish and cowardly
To seed and meet a son of mine
Or too spiteful toward myself
To continue an otherwise strong line
Maybe that's why - All this trying
Is just me still trying to hide, right
Where there's nothing left to hide behind
Heart full of blood, but I'd
Just assume let it dry
Before letting it spill and
Poison someone else's wine

Tune

That melancholic tune
Ringing near your left ear,
Stuck in the side of your head
You hear it here and there
A certain pitch that resonates
A signal in an embedded wave

Like an old friend that
You don't recognize at first
Humming the undertones of
A song you both remember
From a long time ago, for no
Immediately apparent reason

Then it hits you, the jolt of inertia;
You catch yourself from falling
Right before you fall asleep
The meeting place between
A wide, yet shallow ripple
And the causal, fast-sinking rock
Traveling straight and narrow
Down into beneath you

Maybe it's a subtle note
Or an uninvited update
From an undetected channel
Being installed into your mainframe
And just then, the tune is gone,
Poured out of your right ear,
And you're back up and running
Trying to remember the words,
How the melody goes

AYCEAF

Rich conversation

Over good coffee

An abundance of

Colorful, harmonistic nature

Steady calmness

With a drip of new and

Surprising experiences

Quiet moments, alone

Balanced with memorable

Ones with friends, family

Closeness with chosen God(s)

Healthy, moderate and
Temporary escapism -
That harmless, childish joy

Free-flowing time, plenty,
But certainly not an
Infinite amount

Independence

To know the universal truths
Like love and fear
Inside of a strong heart

A proud death

Days Flicker

Sounds stick to the ceilings
Or drown, out in that old place
Oceanic echoes - those days
Confounding their reflection's feelings

Visions paint with oils
Or smear, into the next room
Rivered audio waves - slow doom
Scattering its memories' spoils

Feelings... well they just leave
Or flee, can't at all see where
Empty parking spots - dusty air
Polluting its inhalers' reprieve

Go outside.

Break-neck trends

status checks and updates

Heart frenzies and fake cartoon faces

Gratification tap-bait friends

Apps with red badge edges

Backend data gathering

Fascist hackers sending

Hate e-blasts

Hashtagged ad placement

Mapped, tracked and traced

Plastic-cased lens flashes

Late DM sends, bad intentions

Then again, let's face it

We've made this web-based bed

May as well lay in its net

Fire & Earth

Feet been planted on the ground
A sturdy bend that won't break
Hands held up high and outward,
Fingers twisted and curled in
Held above in scattered places,
While stretching toes pointed down
Spread and squeeze themselves into
The hot, dry, welcoming earth
That breaks open before them

A comfortable lonesome,
Though close to a few others;
Each with their own tangled roots -
Connected family trees
There's a steady, stoic stance
Found in a managed forest
A war formation, posture
Unwavering and waving
Hello to the gentle wind

Stealthy owls, imposing
Critters and slow poison gone,
The air is still full of clouds;
A veil over the fire,
It suggests a thunderstorm -
Heavenly water, washing
Before the air can be clear,
The fire can re-emerge
And the earth can drink it up

Epilogue

That Not-For-Nothin' Nobody

And so the conversation lingers... quieter now, but still alive within a few remaining orange coals on the back burner.

We peek through the hollow blink of Mors, the faceless observer who never knows a first breath but knows every last one all the same. It watches back in fogged glass, mirroring differences through a practiced, endless stare - a silent acknowledgement that we will one day walk beside one another from this sandbox to the next.

Across the meandering path between now and then, there exists a beautiful tapestry of moments woven together by this natural order; It is both individual and collective, both foreign and familiar - a Rorschach pattern that looks sort of like a burning tree and its sun, a rain cloud and its river, the quinta essentia and its spiral, and so on.

So here's to The Nobody, the silent witness, the mirror, the spiral, the mist and its droplets, the sticks and stones, the spark and what comes next...

The Aether.

About the Author

The experience of life is a miracle, rich with precious moments, enlightening lessons and noteworthy perspectives. I do my best to capture and forward what I can. Finding the right words to do so is a lifelong quest.

Married to the love of my life, well into a good career and fortunate to be part of a strong family core, I'm looking forward to these next middle chapters. I'll let you know what I find out.

Next up: A fiction novel about Death (more entertaining than it sounds) and "Aether", the third and final installment of the ThoughtPose Quintessence Trilogy. Check the website, drewcharleschase.com, for a few sprinkles in between.

Love to all and talk soon,

Andrew

www.ingramcontent.com/pod-product-compliance
Lightning Source LLC
LaVergne TN
LVHW052036080426
835513LV00018B/2351